THE KA'ABA in the courtyard of the
MASJID-AL-HARAM, Mecca.

Library of Congress Cataloguing in Publication Data

Leacroft, Helen
The buildings of early Islam

Includes index.
Summary: Describes the characteristics and uses
of various buildings found throughout the Moslem
world including mosques, palaces, bath houses, and
homes.
1. Architecture, Islamic—Juvenile literature.
[1. Architecture, Islamic] 1. Leacroft, Richard,
joint author. II. Title.
NA380.L42   720'.917'671   76-2463
ISBN 0-201-09446-0

Also by Helen and Richard Leacroft

THE BUILDINGS OF ANCIENT EGYPT
THE BUILDINGS OF ANCIENT GREECE
THE BUILDINGS OF ANCIENT ROME
THE BUILDINGS OF ANCIENT MAN
THE BUILDINGS OF ANCIENT MESOPOTAMIA

In preparation

THE BUILDINGS OF BYZANTIUM

Copyright © 1976 by Helen and Richard Leacroft
First published 1976 jointly by Hodder & Stoughton Children's Books
and Young Scott Books, Addison-Wesley Publishing Company, Inc.,
Reading, Massachusetts 01867, USA.
UK ISBN 0 340 20226 2
USA ISBN 0 201 09446 0

Printed and bound in Great Britain by
Morrison & Gibb Ltd, London and Edinburgh

THE BUILDINGS OF EARLY ISLAM

Helen and Richard Leacroft

HODDER & STOUGHTON

LONDON   LEICESTER   SYDNEY   AUCKLAND
and

ADDISON-WESLEY PUBLISHING COMPANY

ISLAM, one of the great religions of the world, was founded by the Prophet Muhammad in the seventh century A.D. Its holy book, the Koran, provided not only a code for living, but also emphasised the importance of the family as a basis for society. Muhammad was born in Mecca and lived and died in Medina, two small cities in the Arabian desert, but the faith which he proclaimed was to be embraced by peoples as varied as the wandering Bedouin, hill tribesmen, merchants and city dwellers. It captured the great Byzantine and Persian empires, spread east into India and west across north Africa to Spain and France.

In this book we shall see that as people from many countries with differing climates and types of building materials became followers – Muslims – each area produced the variations of buildings, mosques, schools, hospitals and houses best suited to its needs. Some were simple, others magnificent; some were flat-roofed and many were domed; but all had the necessary elements for the faith. The most holy place of Islam, binding all Muslims together, is the Ka'aba (see frontispiece), a shrine in the courtyard of the great mosque of Mecca towards which all Muslims turn five times a day in prayer, and to which each endeavours to make a pilgrimage at least once in a lifetime.

Muhammad's home consisted of an open courtyard in which the household tasks were carried out. Thatched rooms for his wives were built against the outer face of one of the mud-brick walls surrounding the court. When his followers gathered in the open space to listen to and talk with the Prophet and join him at prayers, a shelter – zulla – with palm trunks supporting a roof of palm leaves, was erected to protect them from the burning sun. A further simple shelter – suffa – was provided for the poor. In Muhammad's house can be seen the basic ingredients of a mosque.

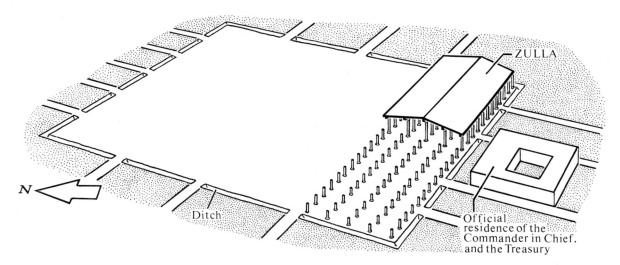

N

ZULLA

Ditch

Official residence of the Commander in Chief, and the Treasury

THE MOSQUE, unlike a modern church, is not just a sacred
building. It is also a place of meeting and rest, and it is closely associated
with the markets and general life of a town. In Kufa, a military settlement, the
courtyard was surrounded by a ditch. The Mecca side of the area was known
as the *qibla*, and here a *zulla* was built. Open on all sides, it consisted of a roof
supported on five rows of tall marble columns which were taken from
deserted buildings. Often early mosques had wooden columns, as shown
below. In this example the qibla has been filled in with a wall.

ESREPOGLU CAMI,
Beysehir, Turkey.
A.D. 696–1297

3

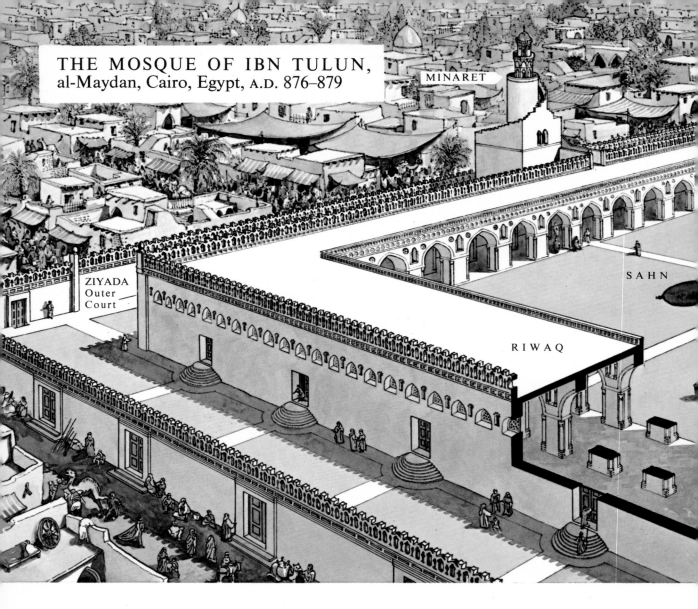

THE MOSQUE OF IBN TULUN,
al-Maydan, Cairo, Egypt, A.D. 876–879

MINARET

ZIYADA
Outer
Court

SAHN

RIWAQ

The Mosque of Ibn Tulun in Cairo, the finest and oldest type of courtyard mosque, was built of brick covered with stucco. To separate the mosque proper from the noise and bustle of the surrounding town, an outer enclosure – *ziyada* – was built around three sides; on the fourth, the qibla side, Ibn Tulun built his *dar* or house. In the middle of the courtyard – *sahn* – stood a covered fountain. Water was sacred to the men of the desert, but in spite of its scarcity, every Muslim had to perform a ritual washing under running water before joining in prayer. Often the fountain in a mosque had to serve as a small town's water supply.

Shady arcades – *riwaqs* – built around three sides of the sahn were covered with flat roofs; the pointed arches, decorated with bands of raised stucco, rested on piers. Each riwaq had two aisles in which Muslims could rest, read or talk with neighbours. The only activities which were forbidden were those which might disturb other people. The sanctuary – *zulla* – had five

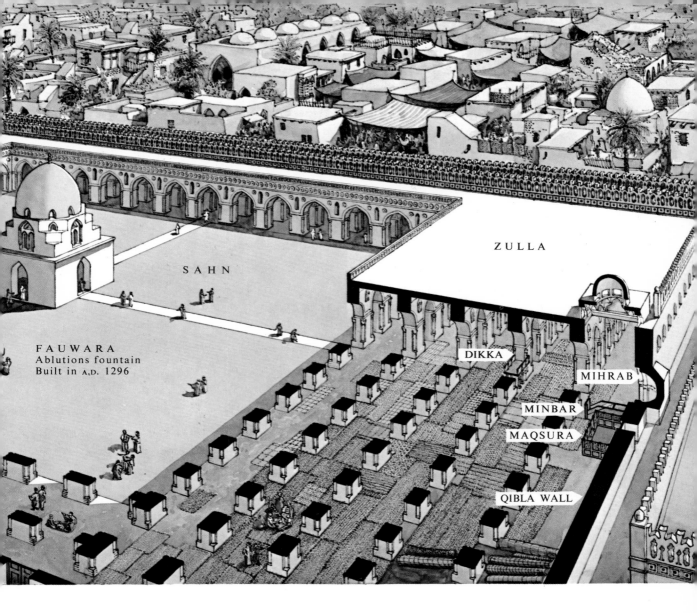

ZULLA

SAHN

FAUWARA
Ablutions fountain
Built in A.D. 1296

DIKKA

MIHRAB

MINBAR

MAQSURA

QIBLA WALL

aisles set parallel to the qibla wall in the middle of which was a niche – *mihrab* – (page 10). The space in front of this was covered by a small dome. The worshippers stood and knelt side by side in straight lines facing the mihrab, of which there was sometimes more than one. The *maqsura* was an open-work screen of either wood or dressed stone. It was first introduced into mosques in the second half of the seventh century to prevent the assassination of the ruler or governor who sat behind it, separated from the rest of the congregation. This separation of the ruler from the people was continued through the centuries, not only in the mosque but later in the palace pavilions, such as the Hall of the Divan at Topkapi (page 28).

A Muslim prayed wherever he might be when the *muezzin's* call came from the tall *minaret* (page 11). On Friday, however, everyone had to attend the mosque and listen to a sermon. This was given by the preacher who sat on the second step of the *minbar* (page 10).

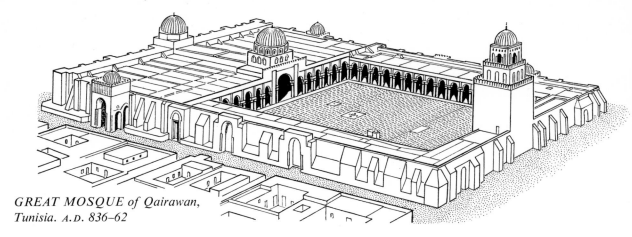

GREAT MOSQUE of Qairawan,
Tunisia. A.D. *836–62*

As the number of people to be accommodated in a sanctuary grew, it had to be enlarged. In the Great Mosque of Qairawan, the sanctuary is almost double the depth of that of Ibn Tulun. It had seventeen aisles running at right angles to the sahn towards the qibla wall, from which the aisles were separated by a wide space. The central aisle was widened and heightened. The arcades, here carried on marble columns instead of brick piers, were given extra stability by means of beams, such as may be seen in the Mosque of Amr, which tied them together in both directions. At Qairawan the space before the mihrab was covered by a large dome. The imposing entrance porch on the façade, facing a minaret, across the sahn was also domed.

The floor of a sanctuary is covered with reed matting or carpets, because during prayers the worshippers have to kneel and touch the ground with their foreheads, so before entering they take off their shoes.

MOSQUE OF
AMR, Cairo,
Egypt. A.D. *673*

6

ULU CAMI, Bursa,
Turkey. A.D. 1396–9

MAUSOLEUM OF
MELIK GAZI,
Kirsehir, Turkey.
c. A.D. 1250

MOSQUE OF ALAEDDIN BEY,
Bursa, Turkey. A.D. 1335

As the faith spread, mosques were built in countries with different climates and building materials. The Turks, who adopted the faith in the tenth century, built with flat roofs and wooden columns as at Beysehir (page 3). In northern Anatolia, which had dry summers but cold winters, they built in the readily available stone, sometimes using constructional methods which may have been copied from the Byzantines. The open side of the zulla facing the courtyard was closed. Often the courtyard disappeared altogether, although sometimes a remnant was left in the form of an opening in the roof of the centre aisle, beneath which a fountain was placed, as in the Ulu Cami (pronounced jami) at Bursa. Where the rainfalls were heavy, flat roofs were unsuitable, so buildings were covered by a single large dome as at Alaeddin Bey, or like the Ulu Cami where twelve stone piers carry arches dividing the building into twenty areas, each covered by a small dome. In an enclosed building windows were needed, and these were placed in the side walls, and also in the drums supporting the domes (page 14).

In many Muslim countries it was not customary to mark burials, but some Eastern peoples continued to erect shrines such as the Mausoleum of Melik Gazi. The body was placed in a crypt, and above, a flight of steps led to a memorial and a place for prayers. The building was roofed by a cone, beneath which was a dome, the religious symbol representing the heavens. This was an early religious idea in the East.

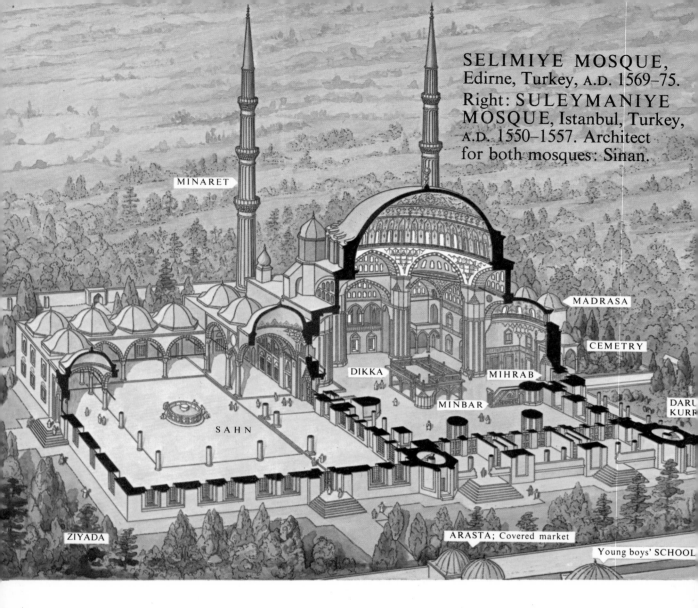

SELIMIYE MOSQUE, Edirne, Turkey, A.D. 1569–75. Right: SULEYMANIYE MOSQUE, Istanbul, Turkey, A.D. 1550–1557. Architect for both mosques: Sinan.

MINARET

MADRASA

CEMETRY

DIKKA

MIHRAB

MINBAR

DARUL KURR

SAHN

ZIYADA

ARASTA; Covered market

Young boys' SCHOOL

In A.D. 1453 the Turks captured Constantinople, where the Sultan set up his capital, and as was often done in the countries which they conquered, the Sultan turned the great church of Hagia Sophia into a mosque. This building was to inspire many architects, including Sinan, who was the greatest Muslim architect of the sixteenth century. In the Suleymaniye Mosque Sinan used an arrangement of domes and half domes similar to that which had been used in Hagia Sophia (see *The Buildings of Byzantium* –

forthcoming), but it had a square plan and so produced a cubic volume. His most important building was the Selimiye Mosque at Edirne, for which he wanted to build an even larger dome than that at Hagia Sophia, so he arranged the piers supporting the domes in an octagon, setting them back against the walls to create a great open space in the central area. Around the mosque were a school for young boys, a madrasa, the house for the readers of the Koran – *Darul-Kurra* – and the market.

8

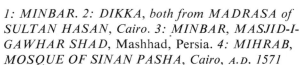

1: *MINBAR*. 2: *DIKKA, both from MADRASA of
SULTAN HASAN*, Cairo. 3: *MINBAR, MASJID-I-
GAWHAR SHAD*, Mashhad, Persia. 4: *MIHRAB,
MOSQUE OF SINAN PASHA*, Cairo, A.D. 1571

INSIDE A MOSQUE

Only essential items are to be found in the prayer hall of
a mosque. The mihrab indicates the direction of Mecca,
to which Muslims must turn to pray. This focusing of
attention in the same direction while at prayer has had a
unifying effect upon Islam. The first mihrab was
introduced in the eighth century into the mosque at
Medina. These niches can be plain or decorated with
coloured marble and stucco work.

The high, raised pulpit with a flight of steps is called
the minbar, and from here the Friday sermons are
preached. Its origin is said to be the three-stepped chair
on which Muhammad used to sit so that everyone could
see him when he was talking to them. It became a
symbol of authority, and rulers received the allegiance
of their followers while seated on it. Minbars have been
built of wood, stone, marble and alabaster, and are
often covered with elaborate decoration.

The *dikka* is a free-standing platform made of wood
or marble, supported on columns and reached by a
ladder. During prayers various movements have to be
made simultaneously by the worshippers, so some of
them go up on to the dikka from where they can see the
leader – imam – and follow his actions; the congregation,
in turn, follow them so that there is perfect timing.

GREET MOSQUE, *Samarra,*
Iraq. c. A.D. *847*

MOSQUE OF HASAN,
Rabat, Morocco. A.D. *1196*

MINARETS

When Muhammad first instructed his followers there
was no call to prayer. But as the Jews used the ram's
horn and the Christians used a clapper, Muslims soon
followed their example, and a call was therefore given
from the highest roof of a building in the neighbourhood
of the mosque.

   The first example of a special minaret was to be
found when the Mosque of Amr was rebuilt in Egypt.
The Caliph, who ordered the rebuilding, ruled from
Damascus, where the Muslims had built a mosque
within a classical temple which had square towers at the
four corners. This may be the reason that the square
shape was adopted. Later towers often had several
storeys and were topped by a small domed chamber.
The minaret of the Great Mosque of Samarra in Iraq
was circular with outside stairs spiralling around it. This
idea may well have been copied from the ziggurats of
Ancient Mesopotamia. From these two basic ideas, the
tall square and the slender round minarets developed,
decorated with carving, glazed tiles or gilding.

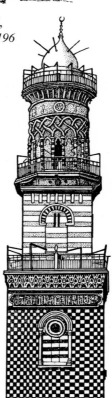

KADHIMAIN MOSQUE,
Baghdad, 15th c. A.D.

MADRASA OF SULTAN
QALA'UN, *Cairo.* A.D. *1285*

11

MASJID-I-JAMI, ISFAHAN. In early times the mosques in Persia followed the pattern of buildings such as the mosque of Ibn Tulun (pages 4–5). But when Persia was conquered by the Seljuk Turks in the eleventh century, they developed mosques which repeated the design of the iwan-halls of the earlier Sassanian palaces (page 22). An inscription in a type of Arabic writing – *kufic* – placed around the drum over the mihrab of the Masjid-i-Jami states that it was erected for

Malik Shah. Built about A.D. 1080, it was on the site of an earlier mosque, some traces of which can still be seen. The word Jami indicates a large mosque used for the Friday services and sermons. Around the courtyard was a two-storeyed arcade, and in the middle of each side, opening on to the courtyard, was an iwan-hall, roofed with complicated stalactite vaulting (page 15). The largest iwan was on the south-west and formed a prayer hall which led into a domed sanctuary in front of the mihrab and

qibla. Beside the sanctuary was a series of rooms and corridors covered by small domes, serving as meeting places, libraries and offices.

Unlike the various Christian groups each of which has its own particular church, all Muslims pray together. However, as in most religions different sects developed within Islam; the Persians belonged to the Shi'ite sect, and the Turks and Arabs to the Sunnite sect. This may be why the iwan-hall type of mosque was developed in Persia, allowing each group to hold separate discussions and meetings in the iwans set on either side of the courtyard.

Another feature to be found in Persia is the large frontispiece – *pishtaq* – a tall rectangular brick frame which surrounds the iwan opening (see cover). These frames and the wall surfaces are decorated with glazed brick or tilework showing abstract patterns or quotations from the Koran. Domes were decorated in a similar manner, or they were gilded as in the holy cities of Jerusalem or Kadhimain, Baghdad (page 11).

13

MOSQUE OF SINAN PASHA,
Cairo. A.D. *1571*

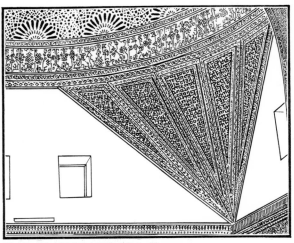

KARATAY MADRASA, Konya,
Turkey. A.D. *1251*

SQUINCHES & DOMES

A problem, which any builder wishing to put a circular dome over a square plan had to face, was how the two could be fitted together. Early attempts were made by covering the angles of the square with slabs, so producing an octagon of irregular shape. On this two courses of stones were laid, the upper projecting slightly in front of the one below; then it was possible to use the structure as the base for a dome. In the fifth century the Sassanians and the Byzantines had used the squinch, an arched vault or half-dome, which was placed across the corner angle; this method of construction was followed by the Muslims, as may be seen above. The Muslims, however, developed the squinch in decorative ways, and at the Friday Mosque in Cordoba, it can be seen scalloped into shells representing the sun's rays.

The Turks made use of elongated triangles in the corners, which, built in brick, could either be left plain or decorated with faience mosaics. Another way of converting a square into a circle was by using *maqarnas*, rows of upright pointed niches which rose one above the other until the circle was complete (pages 12–13). The name stalactite is often applied to these niches, as they seem to be hanging in space.

Domes were constructed of wood or brick, plastered

SULEYMAN 1 MOSQUE, Istanbul,
Turkey. A.D. *1550–7*

THE GREAT FRIDAY MOSQUE,
Cordoba, Spain. A.D. *961–8*

14

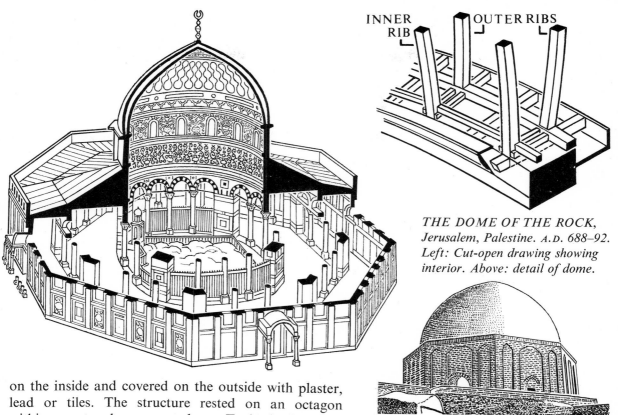

OUTER RIBS

*THE DOME OF THE ROCK,
Jerusalem, Palestine. A.D. 688–92.
Left: Cut-open drawing showing
interior. Above: detail of dome.*

*MASJID-I-JAMI, North dome.
A.D. 1088, Isfahan, Persia.*

*GUR-I-MIR. TOMB OF TIMUR,
Samarkand, U.S.S.R. A.D. 1404.*

on the inside and covered on the outside with plaster, lead or tiles. The structure rested on an octagon within a rectangle, or on a drum. To let in light, the middle of the dome was sometimes left open (page 30), or windows could be pierced in the drum itself (page 31). The Dome of the Rock in Jerusalem, the earliest of Islam's holy shrines, had a double dome of wood, which protected the rock where Muslims believe Muhammad had prayed and ascended into heaven. Each skin of the dome was separately braced with a framework of timber ribs. The outer skin was covered with boards to which gilded tiles were attached. The inner skin had a backing of palm fibre glued to boards and a coat of plaster laid on it, which was then painted and gilded so that it glistened in the sun.

Over the tomb of Timur, the use of two domes was developed to the point where they were of different shapes. The outer dome blended with the exterior of the building, while the inner one exactly suited the interior. The north dome of the Masjid-i-Jami at Isfahan, a single shell dome, is, perhaps, the most perfect dome ever built.

15

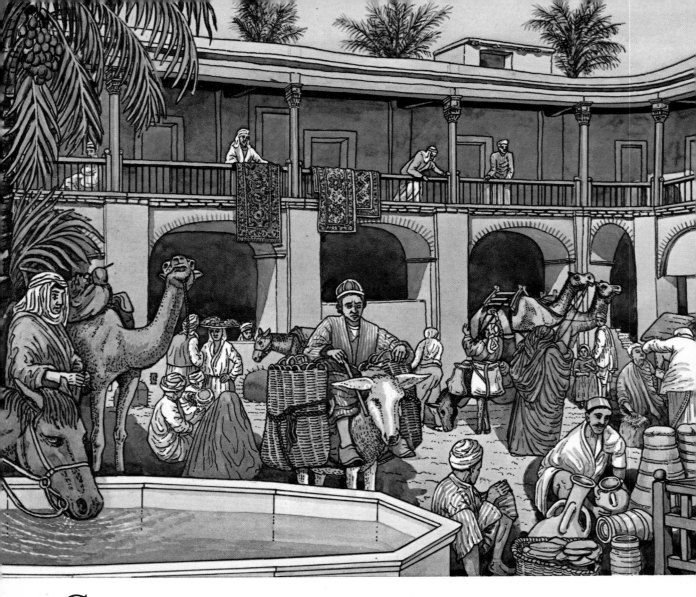

CARAVANSERAI.

Crossing the whole of the Muslim Empire were trade routes used by merchants and officials carrying imperial documents. To provide accommodation at night, *caravanserais* or *khans* were built along the routes, each at a distance of a day's journey. Those called Sultan Khans were built by rulers, who did not charge the people using them; hospitality has always been considered important to Muslims.

The caravanserai was surrounded by a high plain wall which served as a protection in times of war or against brigands. One strong gate, faced with cut-stone blocks, was set in a gatehouse where there were rooms for the innkeeper. Passing through the gatehouse, the travellers entered a courtyard around which were storerooms where the merchants could keep their goods in safety, stables and food stores for the animals, a blacksmith's and a coffee shop. The travellers lodged on the upper floor, the wealthier ones in private rooms, each with its

own hearth; the others in dormitories. Bathrooms and lavatories were provided. In the middle of the courtyard there was often a small mosque raised up on arches so that it was above the general bustle and comings and goings; beneath the arches might be the ablutions fountain. Sometimes stairs led up to the flat roofs which could be used for communal prayers. In larger establishments (page 18) an inner gateway led from the courtyard into a covered hall which was used during the winter; here vaulted apartments were set along either side of a central corridor, in the middle of which was a dome with an opening at the top to admit light and provide ventilation. In some winter halls there were open fireplaces on which food could be prepared. In smaller caravanserais there was no courtyard and the gateway led straight into a hall with columned arcades, around which, at ground level, were corridors where the animals were tethered, and above were sleeping benches for the travellers.

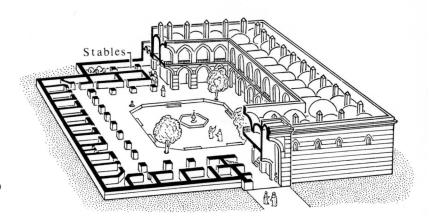

BEY KHAN, Bursa, Turkey.
Early Ottoman period. c. A.D. *1339*

In Persia the caravanserais, some of which were very large with many attendants to serve the travellers, had a blank outer wall with one entrance gate leading into a courtyard surrounded by open arcades, sometimes two rooms deep. Often there was an iwan in the middle of each side of the courtyard following the pattern of the palaces and mosques. As a man's livelihood, and in the desert areas even his life, depended upon his animals, the stables were completely separate from the merchants' quarters. There was no access to them from outside, the only way in being through a narrow passage which led off the courtyard, so that it was impossible for the animals to be stolen.

In large cities, market khans were built in the business areas and stood in rows on either side of one of the main streets. Each khan, or group of khans, was associated with one particular trade; for example: silks, cloth, furs, saddles, or food produce such as rice or salt. Here the merchants stored and displayed their goods, and buying and selling took place in rooms which were arranged as shops around the courtyards.

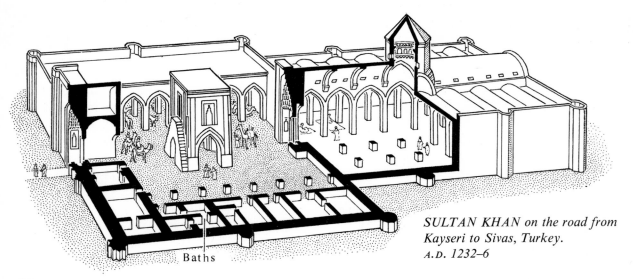

SULTAN KHAN on the road from Kayseri to Sivas, Turkey.
A.D. *1232–6*

Sleeping quarters for each merchant were provided on an upper storey. Every room had carpets or mats on the floor and a hearth; the merchants brought their own bedding with them. When these market khans were built near to a mosque, no special provision for prayer was made, but in the middle of the courtyard there was often a fountain with trees planted round it, and the direction of Mecca was indicated simply by a stone slab. These city khans were built either by the ruler or wealthy men, but, as they were used for trading as well as lodgings, payment had to be made, and the money was used to support the mosques.

When merchants dealt in valuables, such as jewellery and brocades, special provision was made for them in a covered market – *bedesten* – such as that at Edirne. Here strong rooms were arranged on either side of a central covered space, in front of which platforms could be set up for the display and sale of goods. Markets, consisting of shops arranged on either side of an open or vaulted street, were often built beside mosques for which they also provided a source of revenue (pages 8 and 33).

MISR CARSISI. Egyptian Bazaar, Istanbul, Turkey. A.D. 1660

SHOPS

STRONG ROOMS

BEDESTEN, Edirne, Turkey. A.D. 1417–18

19

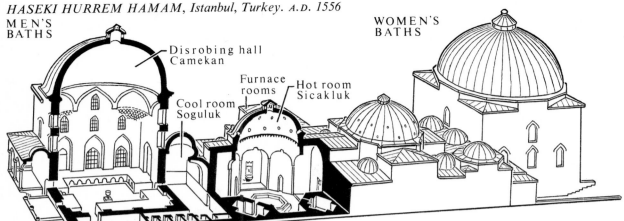

HASEKI HURREM HAMAM, Istanbul, Turkey. A.D. *1556*

MEN'S
BATHS

WOMEN'S
BATHS

Disrobing hall
Camekan

Furnace
rooms

Hot room
Sicakluk

Cool room
Soguluk

WATER. One of the most important buildings in a town was the *hamam* or bath house, which might sometimes be attached to a mosque, khan or bazaar. Immediately inside the entrance was a large dressing room covered with a dome. In the middle of the floor a marble basin collected water from the jets of a fountain. Around the room were benches covered with mats on which the bathers sat to undress, and where they left their clothes in neat piles. Covered with a towel, they walked into the first room of the bath. Here, in a pleasantly warmed atmosphere, attendants massaged and shaved the bathers; they then washed them by throwing bowls of water over them. The water came from pipes, one for cold and the other for hot, which flowed into marble basins, the overflow seeping away through holes in the marble floor. The bathers then entered very hot rooms, the only light coming from glazed holes set in the thickness of the dome. After a session in the heat the bathers returned to the warm room for a time to relax and talk with their friends before dressing and leaving the building. The water and rooms were heated in a manner similar to those of the Romans (see *The Buildings of Ancient Rome*, pages 24, 25, 35), but unlike the Roman bath, there was no pool for swimming. Muslim religious ritual lays down that all washing must be done under running water, and it was considered unclean to share water with anyone else, such as happens in a swimming pool. Separate accommodation was provided for men and women, but the baths were similar and were often set side by side so that the heating arrangements could be shared. Another form of bath was used for medical purposes only; the patient would sit in a circular pool which was filled with running water from natural hot springs.

DRINKING FOUNTAIN.
Hekimoglu Ali Pasha Complex,
Istanbul, Turkey

20

INTERIOR OF WOMEN'S BATHS.
(*After an early manuscript*)

Aqueducts or underground pipes brought water to the towns, where it was stored in cisterns. In Istanbul the aqueduct, built by the Byzantine Emperor Justinian in the sixth century B.C., continued to be used. The people fetched their water supply from public fountains, usually set into the outer wall of a building, with storage tanks behind them fed from the main cisterns. The fountains had a jet and basin often set within an arch, the stone façade being decorated with carvings. Wealthy people had storage cisterns in the basements of their houses to feed their own private fountains. In small settlements the only water supply was often that provided in the mosque. Fountains and troughs for the animals to drink from were provided at intervals along the caravan routes.

Bridges were built at important crossings of the rivers. In the sixteenth century the architect Sinan was responsible for building many stone bridges, their structure being worked out mathematically to make sure that they could withstand the currents when the waters rose up to flood levels. Some bridges were constructed with two tiers of arches and had buildings in the middle and at both ends; sometimes there were shops, and even mosques and caravanserais were to be found.

KHAJU BRIDGE, Isfahan, Persia. A.D. 1642–66

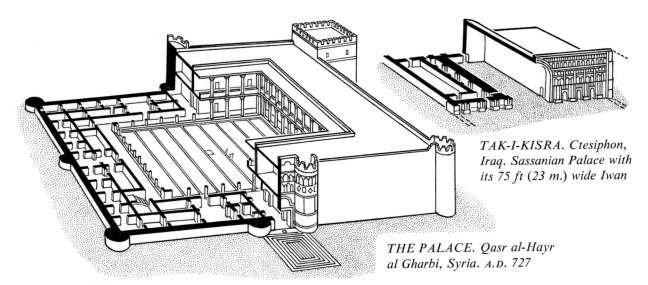

TAK-I-KISRA. Ctesiphon,
Iraq. Sassanian Palace with
its 75 ft (23 m.) wide Iwan

THE PALACE. Qasr al-Hayr
al Gharbi, Syria. A.D. 727

PALACES AND HOUSES. In the early days of Islam
when most of the followers were nomadic, living in tents and wandering from
place to place, the leaders did not need a palace either as a dwelling or for
administration. But when in A.D. 661, the foundations of an empire had been
laid, a palace, where the ruler could be protected from attacks and from which
he could govern, became essential. The final conquest of Persia and Iraq in
A.D. 637, including the sacking of the Sassanian palace of Ctesiphon, may have
inspired the Caliphs, the religious leaders, to set up buildings for themselves.

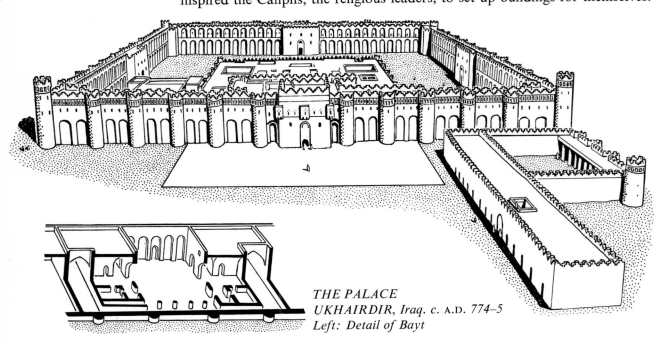

THE PALACE
UKHAIRDIR, Iraq. c. A.D. 774–5
Left: Detail of Bayt

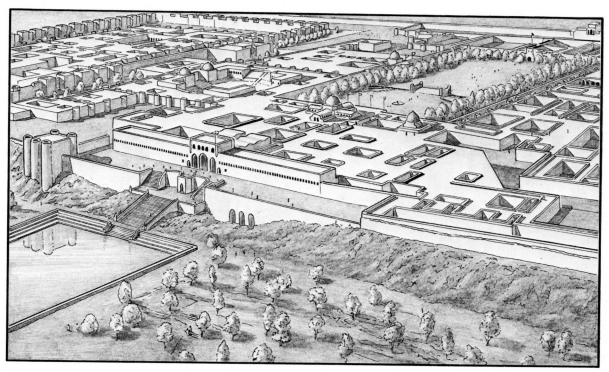

JAUSAQ AL-KHARQANI, Samarra, Iraq. A.D. 836

The earliest form of palace was simply an audience hall for the Caliph, around which his followers lived in tents. The whole surrounding area was laid out as gardens and hunting preserves and enclosed by a wall. As nomadic habits died, the retainers and their families were provided with separate apartments – *bayts* – such as those at Ukhaidir (page 22). Each was basically an iwan with rooms on either side. The bayts were placed around a courtyard, which had only one entrance gate with a domed chamber over it.

As court ceremonies developed, so did the palace. At Ukhaidir a fortified palace was built around a great Court of Honour; on the south side was an iwan-hall with an arched opening framed by a pishtaq (page 13). Here the Caliph appeared for public audiences; private audiences were held in the rooms on either side. His living quarters were set behind, and the whole was surrounded by a corridor which could be guarded. The courtiers lived in the bayts on the eastern and western sides of the Court. A mosque was included within the enclosure.

In A.D. 836 the Caliph moved his capital from Baghdad (page 35) to Samarra, where there was room to spread out the buildings. Here a great flight of marble steps led up to a triple-arched gate where public audiences were given. Behind this was the throne room surrounded by four iwans. The Caliph was now receiving the highest honours.

23

THE ALHAMBRA PALACE,
Granada, Spain, begun A.D. 1230.
Right: Hall of the Ambassadors,
ALCAZAR, Seville, Spain, 12th. c.

Long before the Turks had moved into south-eastern Europe, Muslims had made their way into Spain, which, until it was reconquered by the Christians in A.D. 1492, was to become the meeting place of eastern and western ideas. In the Alhambra at Granada are the best preserved Islamic palaces still in existence. The name Alhambra means the red castle, and it was so called because of the iron oxide in the soil. This, mixed with quicklime, made the tapia of which the walls were constructed. Built on the summit

of the hill called Asabica, the Alhambra was fortified by walls and towers, and within these fortifications the palaces were built. Unlike western palaces which usually consisted of a single unit, Muslim palaces of the Middle Ages were made up of several units (pages 28–29). Each surrounded a court in which were pools of water or fountains to cool the air and delight the inhabitants, such as the Court of the Myrtles (A). At the far end of this court, an arcade, with delicate round-headed traceries set

beneath lintels, leads into the great Tower of the Comares (B), where the Hall of the Ambassadors or Throne Room is to be found. The walls were richly decorated with coloured plasterwork, the windows fitted with coloured glass and great curtains hung by the door. The baths (C) formed part of the *Harem* (D), the completely separate women's quarters.

Set on an axis at right-angles to the Court of the Myrtles is the Court of the Lions (E). Four channels of water lead from the fountain in the middle, where jets of water pour from the mouths of sculptured lions. The court is surrounded on all sides by arcades behind which are living apartments, and at each end there is a pavilion. As there is no direct communication between the two great courts, it may be that the Court of the Lions was for the ruler's private use, and the public entered only into the Court of the Myrtles. Beautiful gardens, planted with trees, shrubs, flowers and playing fountains, were set close by (page 27).

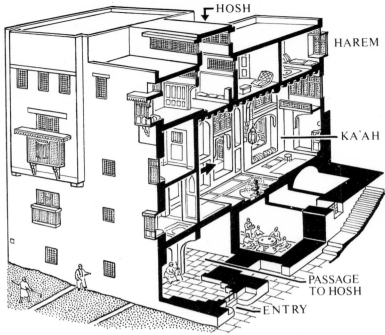

CAIRENE HOUSE, view of Court – hosh – from Maqad, with Musharabiya.

HOUSE – now Gayer Anderson Museum, Cairo.
Above: cut open drawing showing the interior of house. Below: view in the Ka'ah (see arrow above).

Like a mosque, the Muslim house was built to suit the climate and take advantage of available materials. As family life was also closely bound up with religion, the design altered little over the centuries. The Koran laid down that Muslim wives should be invisible to all men except their husbands. In the houses of the wealthy, sometimes two or three storeys high, the entrance door was guarded by a keeper who sat on a stone bench – *mastaba* – set just inside the door, in a passage with one or two turnings to prevent passers-by from seeing in. The passage led into an open courtyard – *hosh* – around which were kitchens, quarters for the servants and also stables for the animals. The principal room or Hall of Ceremonies was the *ka'ah* where the master received his guests. The central area of the floor – the *durka'ah* – would be paved with marble and tiles, making a pleasant pattern; a fountain played into a shallow basin, the water being drained off by a pipe. On either side the

26

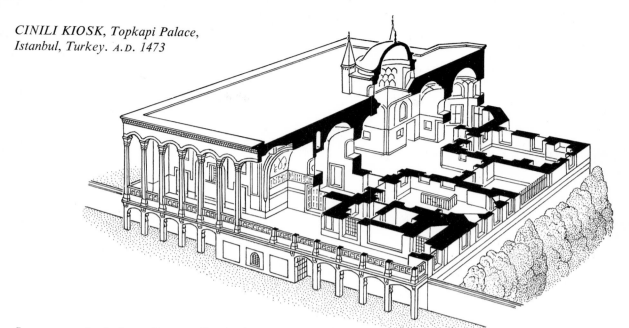

CINILI KIOSK, Topkapi Palace, Istanbul, Turkey. A.D. *1473*

floor was raised about four or five inches (ten to twelve centimetres) to form a paved platform – *leewan* – which was covered with mats in the summer and carpets in the winter; shoes were always removed before stepping on this. In recesses or on the floor were the *deewans*, or divans, consisting of mattresses with cushions leaning against the plastered and whitewashed walls. Any windows there were on the ground floor were set high up and had small wooden gratings.

In the private rooms upstairs, the harem, the windows projected about one and a half feet (forty-six centimetres) out over the ground floor and were fitted with very close lattice work – *musharabiya*. This allowed the women of the family to see the life going on in the streets, without being seen themselves. The main apartment was, like the ka'ah, a large room with leewans on either side of the door. There was no fireplace; when heating was required charcoal was burned in a brazier. Meals were taken from a round table set on a low stool, everyone sitting on the floor. There was a bathroom and latrine. The bedrooms had carpets on the floor, and the beds, consisting of mattresses, would be rolled up during the day. They could also be used on the flat roof at night during the summer months. Many houses had a ventilator on the roof, open to the room below and facing north to collect the cool breezes.

COURT OF THE POOL, GENERALIFE, Alhambra, Granada, Spain

27

THE HAREM
A: Hospital. B: Dormitory of the
Women slaves. Apartments of;
C: Head laundress. D: Kahya Kadin.
E: Head nurse. F: Courtyard of the
Women slaves. G: Dormitory of the
Black Eunuchs. H: Courtyard of the
Black Eunuchs. I: Apartment of the
Aga of the House of Felicity

STABLES AND HARNESS ROOM

THE HAREM

KIOSK OF
OSMAN III

THRONE ROO
OR SULTAN
HA

BEDR
OF MU
III

ROOMS OF
THE VALIDE
SULTAN

HALL OF THE
HEARTH

MOSQUE OF
BESIR AGA

COURT OF THE
HALBERDIERS

ROOMS
OF THE
KADIN

A
MOS

COUNCIL
CHAMBER

TREASURY

QUARTERS OF THE
CHIEF EUNUCH

THE MIDDLE
GATE OR
GATE OF
PEACE

SECOND COURT

GATE OF
FELICITY

QUARTERS OF THE
WHITE EUNUCHS

KITCHENS

ROOMS FOR THE
MEMBERS OF THE
KITCHEN STAFFS

Twenty years after the conquest of Constantinople, which the Turks called Istanbul, the building of new palaces began. So much new building and rebuilding has continued over the years that the buildings which visitors to the Topkapi Palaces see today date from the fifteenth to the nineteenth centuries. The Topkapi palaces were composed of separate pavilions and kiosks, such as the Cinili Kiosk (page 27), set in courts, gardens or around pools and fountains.

Constructed on the site of the acropolis of ancient Byzantium, the vast area of the Topkapi was surrounded by a defensive wall within which lived a population equal to that of a small town. There were several courtyards, each serving a particular section of the community. The army used the outer court; the second courtyard contains the Hall of the Divan, where councils of state were held. The people gathered here to present petitions to the councillors – *viziers* – and the sultan could watch the pro-

28

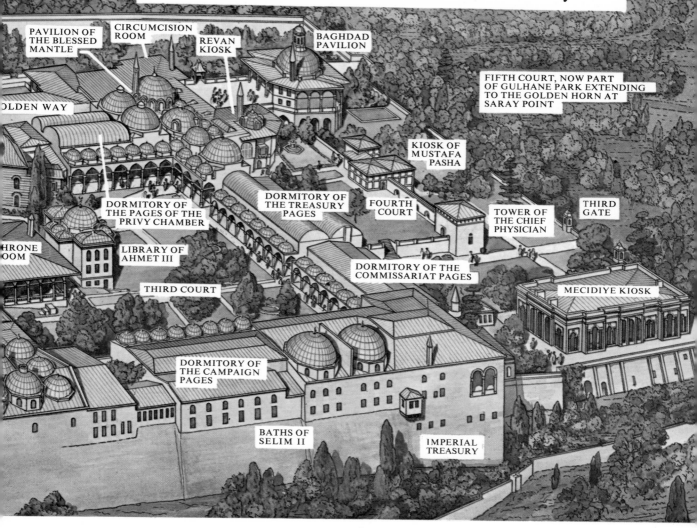

THE TOPKAPI PALACE, ISTANBUL, TURKEY,
from A.D. 1459–65 to the middle of the nineteenth century.

PAVILION OF THE BLESSED MANTLE

CIRCUMCISION ROOM

REVAN KIOSK

BAGHDAD PAVILION

FIFTH COURT, NOW PART OF GULHANE PARK EXTENDING TO THE GOLDEN HORN AT SARAY POINT

OLDEN WAY

KIOSK OF MUSTAFA PASHA

DORMITORY OF THE PAGES OF THE PRIVY CHAMBER

DORMITORY OF THE TREASURY PAGES

FOURTH COURT

TOWER OF THE CHIEF PHYSICIAN

THIRD GATE

HRONE OOM

LIBRARY OF AHMET III

DORMITORY OF THE COMMISSARIAT PAGES

MECIDIYE KIOSK

THIRD COURT

DORMITORY OF THE CAMPAIGN PAGES

BATHS OF SELIM II

IMPERIAL TREASURY

ceedings from an upper grilled window without being seen himself. The great kitchens built by Sinan are also in this court, and they provided meals for five thousand people daily. At the time when a new sultan took power, and for the ceremonies which took place at the end of the month-long fast of *Ramadan*, a golden throne was placed in front of the Gate of Felicity, which leads into the third court. Here are the throne room, libraries, mosques, schools and dormitories for the palace pages, also the sultan's private quarters from which he could approach the harem by a secret corridor. The sultan's wives and the women of the harem, served by many slave girls, were carefully guarded by the Black Eunuchs and strictly ruled over by the *Sultan Valide*, the sultan's mother, who often exercised great power in the Court and Empire. Although the women lived a life of luxury, they were not free, and for many, the only way out of the harem was in a weighted sack which was flung into the Bosphorus.

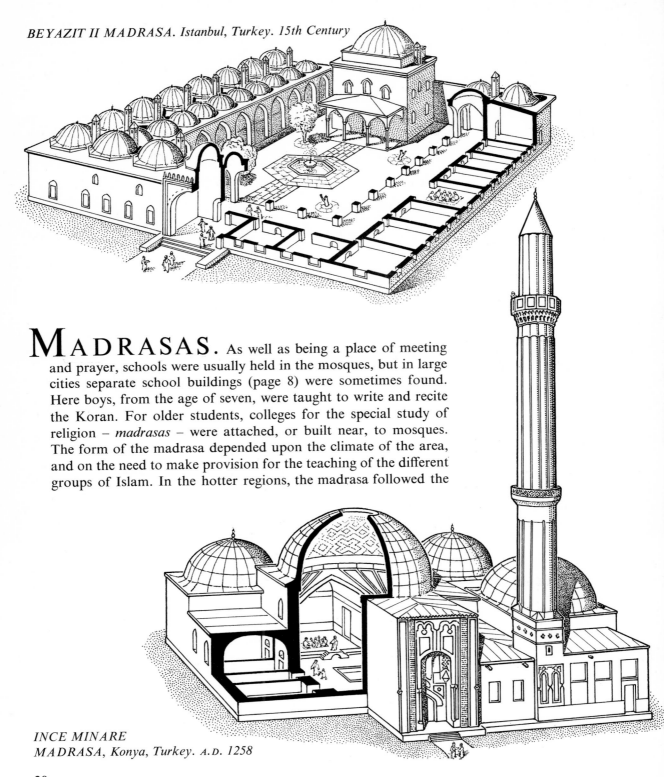

BEYAZIT II MADRASA. Istanbul, Turkey. 15th Century

MADRASAS.

As well as being a place of meeting and prayer, schools were usually held in the mosques, but in large cities separate school buildings (page 8) were sometimes found. Here boys, from the age of seven, were taught to write and recite the Koran. For older students, colleges for the special study of religion – *madrasas* – were attached, or built near, to mosques. The form of the madrasa depended upon the climate of the area, and on the need to make provision for the teaching of the different groups of Islam. In the hotter regions, the madrasa followed the

INCE MINARE
MADRASA, Konya, Turkey. A.D. 1258

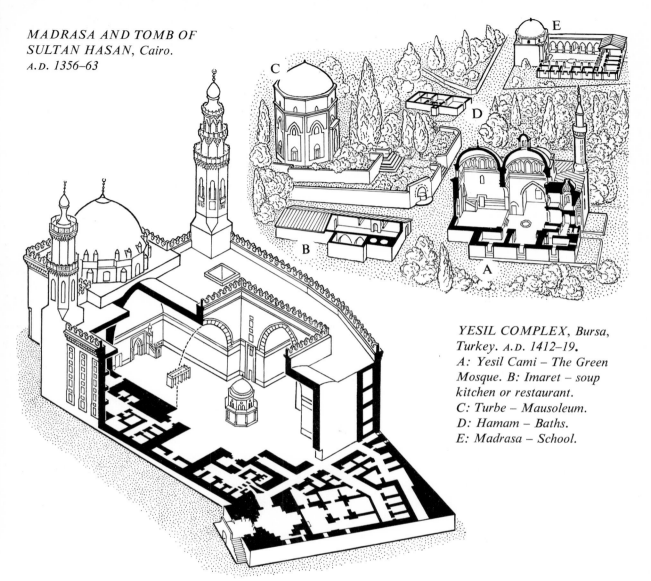

MADRASA AND TOMB OF SULTAN HASAN, *Cairo.* A.D. 1356–63

C

E

D

B

A

YESIL COMPLEX, Bursa, Turkey. A.D. 1412–19.
*A: Yesil Cami – The Green Mosque. B: Imaret – soup kitchen or restaurant.
C: Turbe – Mausoleum.
D: Hamam – Baths.
E: Madrasa – School.*

mosque plan, consisting of an open courtyard with tall iwan-halls set into each side and used as classrooms by the teachers and students. Opening off open arcades, rooms, where the students could live, were provided. Often the tomb of the founder, facing towards Mecca, and a small mosque were included.

The Mamluks, originally from Persia, ruled Egypt from A.D. 1250–1570, and when Sultan Hasan built his madrasa and tomb he used the Persian plan. However, as the building was erected on a restricted site, the courtyard, almost a perfect cube with a fountain in the middle, was here more compact than the Persian examples. Rooms for teachers and students were built into the corners between the iwans. In Anatolia the Seljuk Turks used two forms of madrasa: the open courtyard type, with either open iwans or domed rooms for classrooms, or, in those regions with colder and wetter conditions, the iwan opened off a domed central space, as in the Ince Minare.

31

THE MOSQUE OF AL-AZHAR, CAIRO.
Over the years the madrasas developed in importance, and students followed courses in religion, law – which was based on the Koran – mathematics, astronomy, medicine, literature and history. Highly skilled teachers, scribes, librarians and translators were appointed, and quarters in the madrasas were provided free for them as well as for the students, who, when they had qualified, could themselves become teachers or preachers, leaders of prayer, judges or doctors. So the madrasa became part of a complex of buildings including kitchens – *imarets* – where food was prepared for members of the community, as well as for the poor of the town, and bath-houses. In some cases as many as sixteen madrasas were grouped around a mosque. Gradually, as more and more courses of study were undertaken, some of the madrasas developed into universities.

In the colleges of Baghdad and the great university attached to the mosque of Al-Azhar

in Cairo, which was built in A.D. 970, the later Ottoman university of Istanbul at the Fatih Mosque, and the schools attached to the Suleymaniye Mosque (page 9), scholars gathered students around them for instruction and to conduct experiments. Much of the knowledge of Western Europe is based upon the work of Muslims. In mathematics, the figures or ciphers which are used today were originally introduced by the Arabs. They also discovered the use of algebra – even the name of this study is Arabic –

and it was they who introduced trigonometry. In the universities the study of astronomy made it possible to measure reasonably accurately the length of the year and the time of the equinoxes; to plot out the movements of the stars and the planets. The library of Al-Azhar had some six thousand books in A.D. 1040.

Revenues from markets were used to pay the expenses and to provide the servants needed to run the universities. The Al-Azhar is still today the greatest university in the Middle East.

33

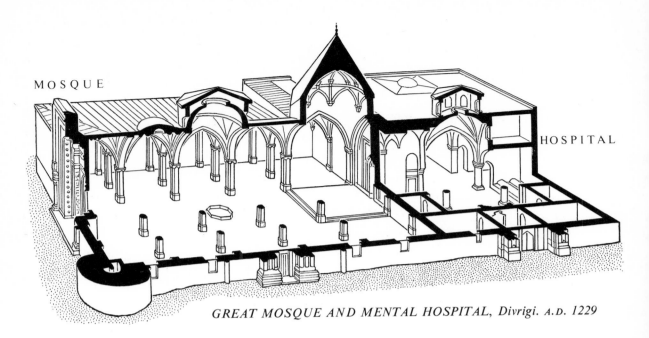

MOSQUE

HOSPITAL

GREAT MOSQUE AND MENTAL HOSPITAL, Divrigi. A.D. 1229

HOSPITALS.

The Koran required all Muslims to show care for those who were sick in body or mind. A hospital was often built beside a mosque, as at Divrigi, above. Hospital plans followed those of the madrasas, with iwans and rooms which were used as wards and for consultations. These were set around either an open courtyard or a covered area lighted by an open eye – *oculus* – which later may have been covered by a lantern. At Edirne, the mental hospital had separate rooms for the patients, and a communal hall with a fountain in the middle and a dais on which musicians played, the music combining with the sound of flowing water. To ensure privacy, hospitals provided for women had an outer, covered, passage leading to the entrance. Medical studies included hygiene, botany and anatomy.

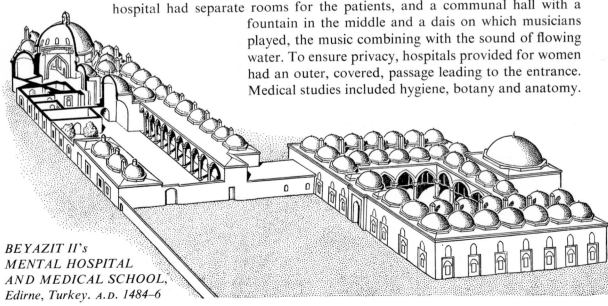

BEYAZIT II's MENTAL HOSPITAL AND MEDICAL SCHOOL, Edirne, Turkey. A.D. 1484–6

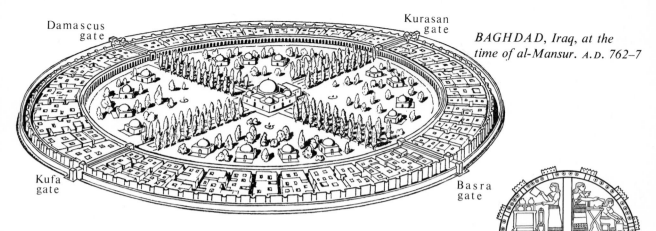

Damascus gate

Kurasan gate

BAGHDAD, Iraq, at the time of al-Mansur. A.D. 762–7

Kufa gate

Basra gate

TOWNS AND FORTIFICATIONS.

In A.D. 754 Baghdad was built as a circular city, perhaps taking the ancient fortified cities of Assyria as a model. The royal palace and the mosque were in the middle in an open space, where the princes' houses and the kitchens were also to be found. Protection was provided by circular walls around which were ring roads leading to the homes of the citizens. Four arcaded ways, with rooms for guards on either side, led to the main gates, which were approached from the city side through a courtyard. Over each of the gatehouses was a domed audience chamber which the ruler used when he appeared to the people. A further courtyard had side openings leading into a dry "moat" where troops could be assembled if there was danger of attack from outside. The moat was surrounded by another wall, outside which was a ditch encircling the entire city.

AN ASSYRIAN FORTIFIED CAMP. Relief from Nimrud, Mesopotamia. 9th c. B.C.

A: The Palace.
B: Mosque.
C: Covered market.
D: Lesser Palace.
E & F: Large and small Baths (hamam).

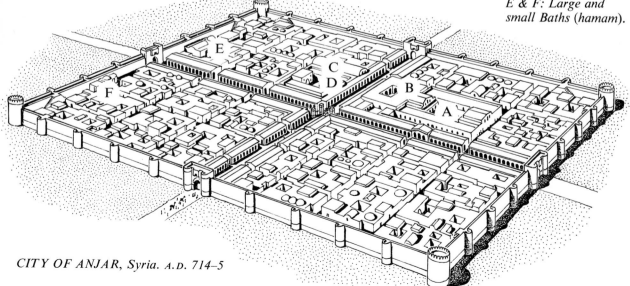

CITY OF ANJAR, Syria. A.D. 714–5

THE DAMASCUS GATE, JERUSALEM.

Cities were walled to provide protection. The gates in the walls gave access to the main roads, which, as at Anjar (page 35), were often laid out on lines similar to a Roman city (see *The Buildings of Ancient Rome*, pages 14–15), with colonnades flanking either side of the roads, and administrative buildings set in the middle of the city. At sunset the gates were closed and were not opened again until sunrise. During the day the areas around the gates were scenes of great activity, with merchants gathering to form their caravans which carried goods to the bazaars of distant cities, and countries as far away as China. From the profits of trading, luxury goods such as porcelain, silks, ivory, gold and spices were brought back to be sold within the Islamic empire. Pilgrims obeying the "Five Pillars of Islam" – faith, prayer, alms-giving, fasting and pilgrimage – met to set out on the pilgrimage – *hadj* – to Mecca. On arrival in the holy city, the pilgrims washed themselves

from head to foot, and having put on special clothing, they went to the *Ka'aba*, a cube-shaped building covered with cloths (see frontispiece). Here they kissed the Black Stone, embedded in the wall beside the door, before walking seven times around the shrine repeating prayers. Other sacred ceremonies took place before the pilgrims set out for home, to be greeted by friends at the city gates amidst great rejoicing.

The castle of the Syrian city of Aleppo (page 38) was strongly fortified against attacks by the Crusaders from Europe, who, in the Middle Ages, attempted to win the Holy Land back from Islam. Dominating the town, it was approached by a steep ramp leading to a bridge over an eighty-foot-wide moat. So that the defenders could not be rushed the passage inside the gate leading to the courtyard had several turns. The castle was planned to withstand long sieges, having deep wells, cisterns, storage chambers and an underground passage leading down to the town.

*THE RIBAT of Susa,
Tunisia. A.D. 771–821.*

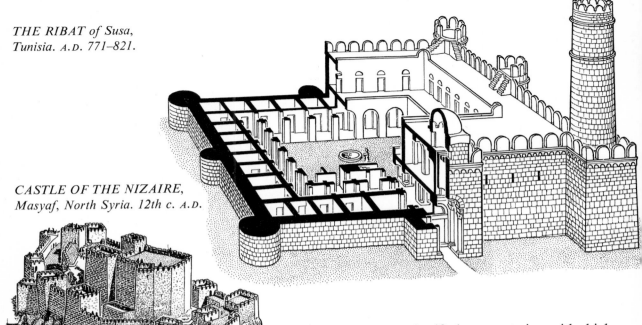

*CASTLE OF THE NIZAIRE,
Masyaf, North Syria. 12th c. A.D.*

*THE CITADEL: gatehouse, bridge and
barbican, Aleppo, Syria. A.D. 1209–12.*

Ribats were fortified monasteries with high watch towers where young Muslims, who were prepared to fight for their faith, studied and lived together. The monasteries were usually built on the outskirts of the Empire in towns on which attacks were likely to be made. Castles, such as that of Nizaire, had towers and protective walling, and it may be that the Muslims copied the great castles which the Crusaders built in the Middle East.

Unlike many of the buildings of the ancient Egyptians, Greeks and Romans which today have disappeared beneath the sands or lie in ruins, most of the many Islamic buildings seen here are still in use, serving the purpose for which they were originally built.

We have looked only at the western part of the early Islamic world, but the faith proclaimed by Muhammad has also grown and spread eastwards into India and beyond. The varied peoples of all the Muslim countries were and still are bound together by the call of the muezzin at daybreak, noon, an hour before sunset, sunset and an hour after sunset, "God is great; there is no other god but God; Muhammad is his prophet, come and pray".

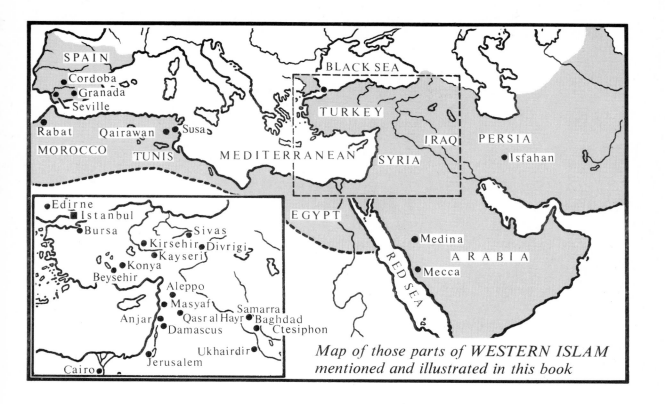

Map of those parts of WESTERN ISLAM mentioned and illustrated in this book

ACKNOWLEDGEMENTS

The authors wish to thank Mrs Olga Ford, Mrs D. Jones, Dr M. A. Ibrahim, Mahmud Al-Hadidi, Curator, Gayer Anderson Museum, and the Director of the Information Office of Turkish Tourism, London, for the loan of materials upon which drawings have been based, also Antony Hutt for comment and criticism during the preparation of the book, and Modjtaba Alavi for translation of Arabic text. They acknowledge their indebtedness to the many authors whose works have formed the background for this study, including: Al-Hadidi, M. *Guide Book to the Gayer Anderson Museum*, Cairo, 1946; Aslanapa, O. *Turkish Art and Architecture*, London, 1971; Briggs, M. S. *Muhammaden Architecture*, London, 1924; Cresswell, K. A. C. *Early Muslim Architecture*, vol 1, parts 1 and 2, Oxford, 1969; Davis, F. *The Palace of Topkapi in Istanbul*, New York, 1970; Duncan, A. *The Noble Sanctuary*, London, 1964; Gabriel, A. *Une Capitale Turque Brousse*, Bursa, vols 1 and 2, Paris, 1958; Golvin, L. *Esai Sur L'Architecture Religieuse Muselmane*, Paris, 1970; Goodwin, G. *A History of Ottoman Architecture*, London, 1971; Grube, E. I. *The World of Islam*, London, 1966; Grury, J. and Jones, O. *Plans, Elevations, Sections and Details of the Alhambra*, vols 1 and 2, London, 1942–8; Hill, D. and Graber, O. *Islamic Architecture and its Decoration*, London, 1964; Hoag, J. D. *Western Islamic Architecture*, New York, 1963; d'Hulst, R. *The Arab house in Egypt*, vol vi, R.I.B.A. Trans., 1890; Jairazbhry, R. A. *An Outline of Islamic Architecture*, London, 1972; Koçu, R. E. *A Guide to the Topkapi Palace Museum*, Istanbul, 1966; Kuban, D. *Muslim Religious Architecture*, Leiden, 1974; Kuhnel, E. *Islamic Art and Architecture*, London, 1966; Lane, E. W. *Manners and Customs of Modern Egyptians*, London, 1836; Le Bon, G. *The World of Islamic Civilization*, Geneva, 1974; Lezine, A. *Le Ribat De Sousse*, Tunis, 1956; Lloyd, S. *Jausaq Al-Khaqani at Samarra*, vol X, Iraq, 1948; Örs, H. *The History of Topkapi Palace*, Apollo, London, July 1970; Ozdes, G. *Turk Carsilari*, Istanbul, 1953; Penzer, N. M. *The Harēm*, London, 1965; Pope, A. U. *Persian Architecture*, London, 1965; Sourdel, D. et J. *La Civilisation de L'Islam Classique*, Paris, 1968; Stewart, D. *Early Islam*, Netherlands, 1971; Tahsin, O. *Topkapi Saray Museum, 50 Masterpieces*, Istanbul; Unsal, B. *Turkish Islamic Architecture*, London, 1970; Vogt-Goknil, U. *Living Architecture—Ottoman*, London, 1966.

39

INDEX

*A MOSQUE
IN MOSUL, Iraq.*

Books by Helen and Richard Leacroft

THE BUILDINGS OF ANCIENT EGYPT

". . . well written and authoritative and covers much in the way of social history. No other juvenile book covering ancient Egypt gives anything comparable to these informative illustrations. . . . Meets curriculum requests for material on architecture of homes through the ages." *Library Journal*

THE BUILDINGS OF ANCIENT GREECE

"It could scarcely be better as a library reference for imaginative and recreative work by the pupils." *The Teacher*

"An informative text complements the excellent illustrations on every page which consist of interpretations of Greek life, mostly in color and precise, carefully labelled drawings showing architectural details. Like the Leacrofts' THE BUILDINGS OF ANCIENT EGYPT . . . valuable in the study of a civilization and of architecture in general." *The Booklist* (*American Library Association*)

THE BUILDINGS OF ANCIENT ROME

"Should be in every school library, if not in every classroom." *School Librarian*

"It is easy to become absorbed in the past, and the Leacrofts present an enticing opportunity to indulge. The superb illustrations of Roman public and private buildings spark the imagination. They lead one to reconstruct the lives of the people. With scrupulous attention to detail the Leacrofts depict the Romans' technological inventiveness, peerless practicality, and adaptive skill . . . its pages are packed with information." *Christian Teacher*

THE BUILDINGS OF ANCIENT MAN

"The text . . . is once again interesting and informative and includes clear explanations of many archaeological and technical terms. This would be a good introduction to the subject for people of nine and upwards." *The Times Educational Supplement*

"The text is well written . . . informative illustrations, many of which are in full color . . . this book is excellent for its information on early buildings and their construction." *School Library Journal*

THE BUILDINGS OF ANCIENT MESOPOTAMIA

". . . The text is clear and efficient. . . . The diagrams are clear, well labelled, and closely fitted to the text. The drawings are also clear and evocative, and the colour spreads are impressive. . . . The publishers must be congratulated on using every square inch of space, end-papers, covers and all, yet without giving the book a cluttered appearance." *The Junior Bookshelf*

ABOUT THE AUTHORS

Richard Leacroft trained as an architect and scene designer and is now Principal Lecturer in the School of Architecture, Leicester Polytechnic. Helen Leacroft trained as an actress at RADA, but later turned to teaching, and now specializes in History and Scripture.

Opposite: Builders at Work. (*After a 15th century mini*

Below: Life in a Mediaeval Village. (*After an early ma*